HISTORY IN FOCUS

Family Life from 1930 to the 1980s

Frances Wilkins

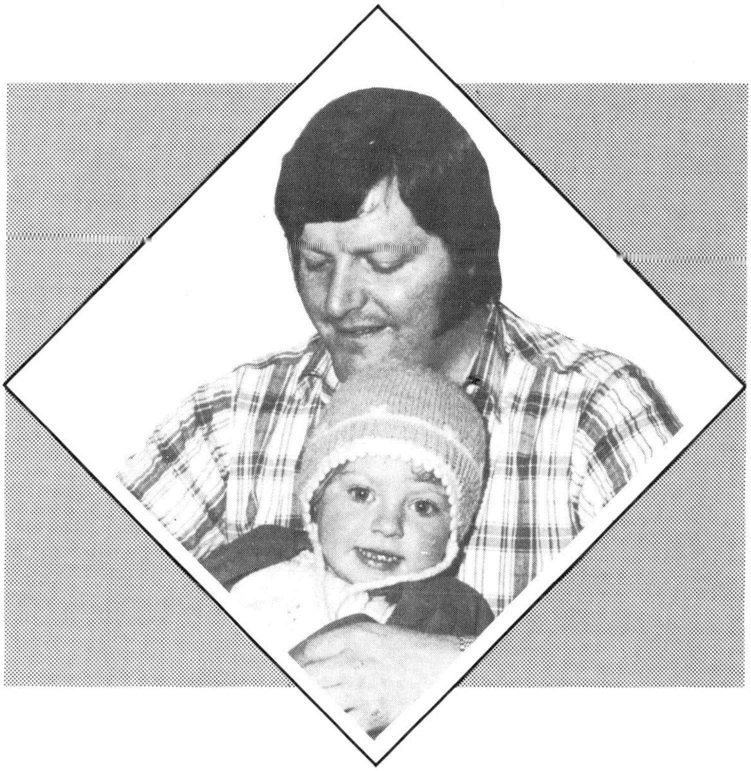

Batsford Academic and Educational London

First published 1985

Typeset by Tek Art Ltd, Kent
and printed in Great Britain by
R J Acford Ltd
Chichester, Sussex
for the publishers
Batsford Academic and Educational,
an imprint of B. T. Batsford Ltd,
4 Fitzhardinge Street
London W1H 0AH

ISBN 0 7134 4818 0

Frontispiece In many families nowadays the father takes an active part in looking after the children (*Barnaby's Picture Library*)

ACKNOWLEDGMENTS

The Author and Publishers would like to thank the following for their permission to reproduce copyright illustrations: Associated Press, figure 60; Barnaby's Picture Library, figures 4, 8, 10, 26, 28, 29, 37, 42, 44, 51, 56, 58 and 59; BBC Hulton Picture Library, figure 36; Batsford archive, figures 1, 24, 41 and 53; Sue Chapman, figures 20, 23, 32 and 47; Children's Film Foundation, figures 39 and 40; GLC Photo Library, figures 9, 13, 15, 21 and 33; Richard and Sally Greenhill, figures 16 and 22; Imperial War Museum, figures 3 and 11; Interquest Association, figure 46; Ron McCormick, figures 19, 27, 38, 55 and 57; Mandel Archive, figures 7 and 18; Mansell Collection, figures 5, 14, 17, 25, 30, 31, 35, 49 and 50; Photosource, figures 2 and 54; Esther Rantzen, figure 12; Michael Ryan, figures 34 and 43; Times Newspapers Ltd, figures 45 and 52; Watford Association Football Club Ltd, figure 48; William Younger & Co. Ltd, figure 6.

Contents

List of Illustrations

1
Changing Times

Families before the War

Father was the head of the family in the nineteen-thirties. This was undisputed in most households, whatever their social position. Although the First World War had done a great deal for women's emancipation it had not appreciably changed the belief that it was the father who should make all the important decisions. The reason was that the father was normally the only breadwinner in the family. Married women very rarely went out to work in the nineteen-thirties. In fact, the only working wives were generally either the very poor, who mostly worked as "chars" (meaning charladies), or women with some special talent, such as actresses and journalists.

1 Perhaps the best-known family of all.

In the nineteen-thirties the average family was very small. It was quite commonplace for parents to have just one child, and only the poor and uneducated had more than two or three. The reason was partly that birth control measures were at last freely available, and partly that people had come to realize that it was a mistake to have more children than they could afford to bring up properly.

Many families found it difficult to support even one child. Unemployment was high, particularly in the industrial areas of the North and in Wales. In 1930 the number of registered unemployed was two million. It soared to two and three quarter million in 1933, and was still one and a quarter million at the outbreak of war in 1939. Moreover, people in work often received pitifully small wages. Civil servants, teachers and the like even had their salaries cut by 10 per cent in 1931. Only in the mid-nineteen-thirties did the country begin to come out of its economic slump, and quite ordinary families were able to consider such luxuries as small cars and holidays on the Continent.

Changes after the War

When war broke out, family life was naturally seriously disrupted. Most young men either volunteered or were called up for the Forces. Women undertook the work which the men had previously done, and the children in the large cities (with their mothers, if the children were under the age of five) were evacuated to the country.

Even when peace returned, family life did not resume its previous pattern. Many

2 The family unit was often broken up during the war, with the father going off to fight and children being evacuated from the cities to "safe" areas.

3 Wartime health poster. People were gradually becoming aware of the lack of health care for the poor and in 1948 the National Health Service was established.

married women were no longer content to stay at home all day, but wanted to continue going out to work. They enjoyed the financial freedom it gave them, and also, with an ever-increasing number of labour-saving devices available, they found that looking after their homes and children no longer filled their whole day. There was a great desire among many families to move into better housing. In 1951 no less than a third of the population was still living in accommodation without even a bath. With two wages a family could sometimes afford to buy their own home, and for those who could not the authorities built large number of new council houses, blocks of flats and even whole new towns.

Women's new financial independence undoubtedly led to more divorces, however. Before the war most women could not have supported themselves or their children if they had left their husbands. By 1947 the number of divorces was ten times higher than in 1939, although this was still a very small number compared with today's figure of one divorce for every three marriages.

Some people thought the increase in divorces was linked to the drop in church-going. Although most babies were still christened, barely 10 per cent of the population attended church on a Sunday by the nineteen-fifties. Worst hit were the Free Churches, while the least affected was the Roman Catholic Church, which had grown in size considerably in Britain, through the influx of foreign immigrants during and after the war.

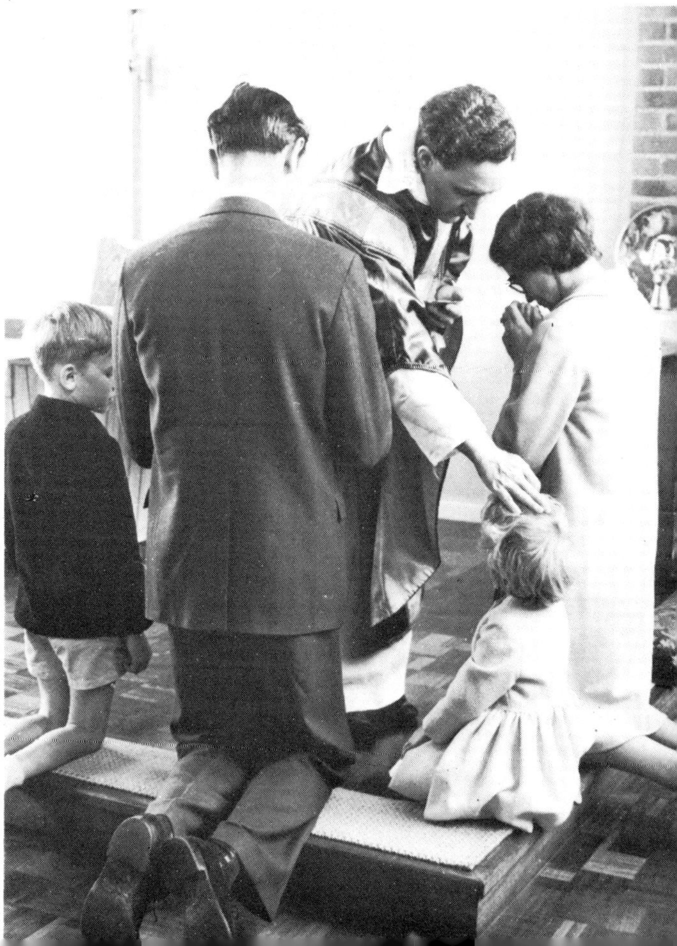

4 Although not nearly as many people go to church now as they did in the nineteen-thirties, family services are still held. This is family communion in a Church of England church. The children have not yet been confirmed, so they receive a blessing.

Improvements in the 1950s

By the nineteen-fifties most families were much better-off than ever before. The Prime Minister of the time, Harold Macmillan, said in 1959 that people "had never had it so good". Children on average were several centimetres taller than their parents, owing to better feeding, and they were also better-educated, as many more were staying on at school to go into the Sixth Form, instead of leaving at the statutary school-leaving age (at that time) of fifteen. There was also much better care available when people fell ill. Before the war the only people who were entitled to receive free attention from their doctors were the poor, who were "panel patients". After the introduction of the National Health Act in 1948, the vast majority of families decided to make use of the free National Health Service, although, more recently, some better-off people have become dissatisfied and have joined various private health insurance schemes.

Immigrants

Britain's prosperity was obviously one reason for the huge tide of immigrants after the war. Thousands of families from the Commonwealth began to arrive, with the hope of raising their standard of living. In 1961 some 120,000 immigrants came to settle in Britain, although the number was considerably reduced after the passing of the new Immigration Act in 1962. Then trouble abroad (such as the expulsion of Asians from Kenya) caused countless other people to remember that they were Commonwealth citizens, with the right in many cases to live in Britain. As time went on, it became increasingly difficult to generalize about family life in some parts of the country where large numbers of immigrants had settled, because every group of immigrants had its own particular traditions and customs.

Mobility in the 1960s

British people themselves were also far from static in the nineteen-sixties. Work was plentiful, and families would often decide to move to another area because there was more money to be earned there. This meant that there was a tendency for people to live further and further from their relations, but at the same time many more of them had cars and telephones than in the past, which enabled them to keep in touch with each other.

The 1970s and 1980s

In the nineteen-seventies the number of unemployed began to rise again rapidly. But families were not usually as badly hit as they had been in the grim days of the nineteen-thirties. Unemployment pay was much higher, and also, as many families had two wage-earners by this time, there was often one wage-packet still coming into the home.

Nowadays family life may seem more hectic and competitive than before the war. Prices and wages are constantly rising, and there is more violent crime. But, generally speaking, most families today are better-housed, better-fed and better-educated than in the nineteen-thirties, and there is more concern for the old, the sick and those in misfortune of any kind.

2
Fathers

The Father's Role in the 1930s

In the nineteen-thirties the average father was still quite clearly the head of the household. But fathers were not usually such frightening and overbearing figures as they had frequently been before the First World War. This changed attitude was largely due to the new place women had in society, but it was also due, to some extent, to a feeling that children should be brought up in an atmosphere of love, and not of fear.

Nevertheless, most fathers would never have thought of giving a hand in the house. They were the breadwinners, and it was the mother's task to do all the domestic work. There was certainly plenty to do, with coal fires to be laid, all the washing to be done by

5 Before the war it was common for men to spend their evenings and spare time with their "mates", leaving their wives at home to look after the children.

6 Many pubs nowadays have a "family room" where children can play while parents drink and eat.

hand, and the need to go shopping almost every day, as there were no deep freezers and very few fridges.

Unemployment

Even unemployed fathers very rarely thought of helping with the housework. And they would certainly never have been willing to be seen pushing a pram in the street. To bring in a little extra money, the wife of an unemployed man would often get a job "charring", but she still had to do all her normal housework as well.

In fact, one of the greatest dangers of unemployment was that it made men unemployable. Many of them just idled their time away, lounging around together at the street corners or in the "pubs". It did not occur to them that if they did not keep their minds and bodies alert and active it would become increasingly difficult for them ever to gain employment again. Most fathers were also unwilling to move home to find a job. (The unemployment chiefly affected South Wales, Lancashire, Yorkshire, parts of the Midlands, North-East England and Clydeside.) Although they might know that they would have a much better chance of finding work in the more prosperous parts of the country, in one of the "new" industries, like car production, they resolutely refused to leave the areas in which they had been born.

Wartime

When the war came, the situation immediately changed. All fit young men were quickly conscripted into one of the armed forces. Even older men, and men in so-called "reserved" occupations, like coal-mining and steel production, were expected to take on some form of war-work, such as joining the Home Guard or fire-watching.

Fathers who did not have to leave home often found their family life disrupted as well. If they lived in a big city and had children less than five years old, their wives might have gone to "safe areas" along with the children. Also, many wives took up war-work in factories and hospitals. In fact, from 1940 onwards childless wives, and wives with grown-up children, were "called up" if they were not already doing some kind of war-work.

7 During the war everyone joined the war effort. Men who had not been called up into the forces were required to do part-time war-work. These two are keeping a look-out on top of a Lancashire cotton mill.

Work after the War

When the war was over there was work for virtually everyone. In fact, industry was crying out for labour, in order to put the country back on its feet again. Also wages in real terms had risen by 50 per cent or more in some trades, so that many families were able to enjoy a higher standard of living than ever before.

There was a significant change since pre-war days in the type of work people were doing. For example, the percentage of men engaged in agriculture was soon little more than 3 per cent of the national labour force. This was because farming had become much more mechanized with the introduction of the new "factory farming" methods, and one man was able to do the work that had required twenty or even thirty men twenty years earlier. On the other hand, the number of people employed in the public sector was rising rapidly. With the introduction of the new "Welfare State" there was an ever-growing demand for more employees to run it. Not only were far more doctors, nurses, teachers, welfare officers and social workers required, but also vast armies of clerks and typists to administer the new schemes.

One of the most noticeable changes after the war was the number of married women at work. It seemed that large numbers of mothers had decided that they liked going out to work and having an income of their own. This in turn changed the pattern of life in the home, as most working mothers expected their husbands to take some share in running the house and looking after the children.

A small proportion of fathers frowned on the idea of their wives going out to work. They thought that their children would suffer if they had to be left with a child-minder, or sent to a nursery. But it soon became clear that there was no evidence that this was harmful, and there was certainly no question that many families benefited dramatically by having not just one wage-earner, but two.

New Unemployment

For twenty years or more the economy continued to flourish. There was virtually no unemployment, and people were able to afford all kinds of new luxuries. For example, in 1960 there was one car for every 9.3 people, but ten years later there was a car for every 4.7, and

▲
8 Fathers today spend more time with their families. They tend to have a closer, less formal relationship with their children than fathers did in the nineteen-thirties.

the number of people going abroad for holidays rose four-fold over the same ten-year period.

Then suddenly in the nineteen-seventies unemployment became a problem again. Within a few years the number of unemployed was as high as before the war, and was still rising. This time, however, unemployment was much more general all over the country, although it still affected the areas where there were heavy industries (like the North Midlands and Scotland) the most.

By the late nineteen-seventies there were more than three million unemployed. A large proportion of these were teenagers, but by far the greatest number were husbands and fathers. Nevertheless, there is probably less hardship today than in the nineteen-thirties, because unemployment benefits, in real terms, are much higher, and in many cases the wives still have a job, which helps the family budget.

Fathers Today

Whether fathers are in work or not, they certainly spend more time with their families nowadays. This is partly because people usually have a much shorter working week and longer holidays than they did in the past. But it is also partly because it has become less common in recent years for men to meet together in the evenings and at weekends while their wives and children stay at home. Before the war, for example, men often spent their spare time with their "mates" in a "pub". But today if a man goes to a "pub" for an evening he usually takes his wife with him. Similarly, the television and the car provide pleasures which a whole family can share, and there is less incentive for a father to spend his leisure time away from his wife and children.

3
Wives and Mothers

Before the War

"A woman's place is in the home." Almost everyone accepted this, at least as far as married women were concerned, before the Second World War. Even women who had spent years in training for a profession found themselves compelled to stay at home, whether they liked it or not, from the moment they were married, as hardly anyone was willing to employ them.

A large proportion of women probably did wish to stay at home. But there must have been many others who (at least secretly) felt bored and frustrated. Most better-off families still had servants to do most of the housework, and even ordinary, middle-class families usually had a "char" who came in for a few hours each week to do the "heavy" work. At the same time, there was usually far less work to do than there had been previously. People

9 A trip to the local laundry in 1931. "Wash-day" nowadays has been made much easier with modern fabrics and washing powders, and many families have a washing-machine in their own home.

10 During the war, when rationing was introduced, it was up to the wife to keep a careful check on the family expenditure.

were moving into more compact, modern houses, and there was an ever-increasing number of labour-saving appliances. Most important of all, people were having fewer children. In fact, the early nineteen-thirties saw the birth-rate drop to an all-time low of less than two children per family on average.

It was only the poorest wives and mothers who usually went out to work in the nineteen-thirties. It was they who did the "charring" to make a little extra money for their families. This was normally the only work they could get, except in the north of England, where there was nearly always a demand for cheap female labour in the cotton-mills and various other types of factories.

Wartime and After

When the war broke out the situation suddenly changed. Mothers with children under five were evacuated from the cities to safe country areas, along with their children. But most other married women took up some form of war-work, either full- or part-time, or took over the jobs of the men who had gone into the Forces. It was an enormous opportunity for a great many women. At last they had the chance to show that they could do many jobs which they had never been allowed to do before. As well as working in factories, women became bus conductresses, post-women, ambulance drivers and even farm-workers as part of the war-time "Women's Land Army".

Women had done many of these jobs in the First World War. But this time it was different. When the Second World War ended, many women refused to go back to staying at home all day. So the government was

11 A wartime poster calling on women to join the war effort. When the men returned from the fighting many women had become used to their independence and chose to continue working.

compelled to provide such things as nurseries for babies and toddlers, and school dinners for older children, so that mothers could continue to go out to work if they wished.

There was little objection by this time to most married women having a job. But many people still thought it wrong that the mothers of pre-school children should not be at home all day. The women's reply to this was either that not all women wanted to be tied to a baby and that they needed other interests, or just that they were desperately anxious to improve their family's financial position.

Domestic Jobs

In contrast to pre-war days, very few women worked as domestic servants after the war. Even better-off families could do most of their housework themselves, with the aid of washing-machines, vacuum cleaners, dish-washers and the like. But there were still a large number of domestic jobs to be had in schools, factories and offices, and, particularly during the tourist boom of the nineteen-sixties and nineteen-seventies, in hotels and guest-houses.

Shops

Many women also went to work in shops after the war. This had always tended to be rather low-paid work, which most men did not want except in a managerial position. But, with the introduction of self-service supermarkets in the early ninteen-sixties, the number of women required in the shops fell considerably, although the women who were still employed tended to earn rather more than before.

Light Industries

On the other hand, many new light industries were set up in the nineteen-fifties and nineteen-sixties. These mostly produced small, but expensive items, such as electronic equipment and, a few years later, computers. The work is particularly suitable for women, whose smaller fingers usually are better than men's for the intricate and delicate operations that this type of production entails.

Women in the Professions

Women rarely obtained what are called "top jobs" in the nineteen-fifties and nineteen-sixties. In fact, very few women even attempted to enter any profession except the traditional ones, like teaching and nursing. This was partly because there was so much discrimination against them, and also partly because it probably never occurred to most of them that they were capable of doing the same type of work as men.

In 1951, for example, there were more than forty-two thousand doctors in England and Wales. Of these, fewer than six and a half thousand were women. Similiarly, out of well over twenty-three thousand lawyers, under seven hundred were women, and out of one hundred and eleven thousand engineers, surveyors and architects, only twelve hundred were women. Even as late as 1964 the situation had barely altered. The proportion of women to men doctors had increased by only one or two per cent. The number of practising women lawyers had actually fallen, and the number of women who were qualified engineers, or in some similar profession, had remained just about the same.

The Sex Discrimination Act

Then in 1975 the Sex Discrimination Act was passed. This has made it illegal to discriminate against anyone on the grounds of sex, which normally means to discriminate against women. But discrimination is difficult to prove, and in any case a woman's education and previous experience often mean that she can only obtain one of the traditional women's jobs. Similarly, women find it difficult to get promotion in most jobs. Employers tend to think that women are unreliable, because of their family commitments, and that they should therefore not be given responsibility.

▲
12 A modern "working Mum" who manages to combine a busy job with bringing up a family. Esther Rantzen with her husband Desmond Wilcox and their three children: Joshua, Emily and Rebecca.

As a result, despite the fact that women, by law, must now be paid the same rate as men, in practice, they earn on average only two thirds as much as the average man because women normally occupy lower positions

The Rise in Divorces

The fact that more women go out to work nowadays is undoubtedly one reason for the rise in divorces. It has given women the means to support themselves and their children if they decided to leave their husbands. But the rise in divorces is also due to the Legal Aid Act of 1960, which helps poorer people to obtain legal advice, and to the Divorce Law Reform Act of 1972, which has greatly simplified the divorce procedure.

4
Children

A Declining Birth-Rate

One of the government's chief worries in the nineteen-thirties was the falling birth-rate. It was only two children per family, which meant that the number of births was barely more than the number of deaths. In fact, one M.P. said that if the birth-rate continued to decline there would be only about five million people left in Britain by the end of the century.

People were determined not to have more children than they could afford, however. This particularly applied to people in the lower middle class, many of whom remembered having been one of a large, poverty-stricken family themselves. They were helped by the new birth-control clinics, which were gradually being opened everywhere with the slogan, "Children by choice, not by chance".

Babies in the 1930s

More than half the babies who were born in the nineteen-thirties were born at home. Mothers were usually taken to hospital only if it was thought there might be complications with the birth. However, most better-off mothers went into private nursing-homes, and paid their own doctor, as well as a midwife, to attend them.

There was no innoculation available for babies, except vaccination against smallpox (this was compulsory by law until as late as the nineteen-seventies). As a result, infectious diseases like whooping-cough, diphtheria, scarlet fever and measles were all rife among children, especially in the poor, over-crowded inner-city areas.

Malnutrition

At least one child in five suffered from malnutrition in the nineteen-thirties. There were no school dinners, and meals at home

13 As part of the Welfare State, milk was given to children at school. This helped to make up for the poor nutritional value of the food many of these children would have eaten at home.
▼

often lacked the expensive body-building foods. Fortunately, there was school milk (free for the poorer children), although some parents were still worried about their children drinking it, in case it was infected with tuberculosis.

Wartime – Evacuees

Then the war broke out. Within a few days three quarters of a million children were evacuated from the forty largest cities in Britain to safe places in the country. Despite this mass evacuation, nearly eight thousand children were killed in air-raids, and almost exactly the same number were seriously injured.

The war did have one good effect, however. Many middle-class women in the "safe areas" were shocked when little girls with no knickers and boys wearing their fathers' old, cut-down trousers were billetted on them. They were even more horrified when they discovered that many of the children were covered with lice and fleas, and that they often shrieked with fear at the unknown experience of having a bath. Naturally, even the better-off had been aware of the hardship and poverty that existed in the nineteen-thirties. But there was quite a difference between reading about such things in the newspapers and actually seeing the results of them in your own home. In fact, there was such an outcry that even in the midst of the war the government was forced to take action, and the result was the drawing up of the various acts which created the new Welfare State.

The Birth Rate Rises

Immediately after the war the birth-rate soared as men came home from the services. In fact, throughout the whole of the nineteen-fifties the number of babies continued to increase. As a result, Britain's population went up by approximately two and a half million, the greatest increase in any period in the country's history. The reason was partly that people were becoming more prosperous. But it was also partly that women were marrying earlier (half the women were married by the age of twenty-five). The size of families has remained much the same, however, through-out all the post-war years. This is about 2.2 children per couple, only slightly higher than in the nineteen-thirties.

Clinics and Vaccination

After the war clinics were opened everywhere, where mothers could take their new babies. There the babies were weighed, and given free orange juice and cod liver oil, and also inexpensive powdered milk, if their mothers wished. Good progress had also been made with vaccines by this time, and they were available for many different crippling diseases, such as polio, whooping-cough and diphtheria.

Dr Spock

One notable change after the war was in the way in which children were treated by their parents. In the nineteen-thirties the emphasis

14 During the war years there was a growing awareness of the need for children to receive regular medical attention. This is a "family consultation" at the Peckham Health Centre where families were invited to have a complete check-up once a year.

had been firmly on children not being spoilt, although discipline was not as strict as in earlier times. But after the war great stress was laid on parental love being constantly demonstrated by cuddling and comforting, and Dr Benjamin Spock's book on bringing up children with love became a bestseller.

A Decline in Infant Deaths

By the nineteen-sixties it was becoming normal for most mothers to have their babies in hospital. The usual time they had to spend there had been reduced, however, from a fortnight to forty-eight hours. By going into hospital the mothers had expert medical attention immediately at hand, and as a result

▲
15 Andover children's home, 1931. In 1948 the new Children's Act required that local authorities make every effort to place orphan children with foster parents so that the children could grow up as part of a family.

the infant death-rate fell to below 2 per cent in 1964, for the first time ever.

Children without Parents

Most children, of course, are born into families where they are wanted. But there have always been some whose parents either could not, or did not want, to look after them. Even in the nineteen-thirties many of these children were adopted, while others were looked after in such

▲
16 These four children, from widely different cultural backgrounds, have formed a new family with their adopted parents. Today it is not easy to adopt a child. A careful investigation is made of the prospective parents to check that they will provide the child with a secure, happy family life.

institutions as Dr Barnardo's, where every effort was made to give the children a happy, stable childhood.

Unfortunately, some children before the war were merely passed from one child-minder to another. Some of these child-minders did the best they could, but others showed the children little or no kindness or affection. As a result, a new Children's Act was passed in 1948, which laid a duty on all local authorities to ensure that proper care was taken of any child, or young person under seventeen, who had no parent or guardian. In most cases, the authorities try to find permanent foster-parents for the children. This is clearly the best substitute for a normal family life, and sometimes even leads to adoption. It does not always prove easy, however, and some authorities have even opened shops recently, where it is hoped that the needs of some of the children may catch the eye of suitable people to foster or adopt them.

The best solution, of course, is to try to reduce the number of unwanted children. This has undoubtedly been helped by the Family Planning Act of 1967, which permits all local authorities to provide birth control services. But even today there are still many children who cannot live with their parents, and about half of these are cared for in institutions and about half by foster-parents.

5
Teenagers

Before the War

Before the war the word "teenagers" simply did not exist. No one thought of the thirteen- to nineteen-year-olds as a special group on their own. Until young people left school at fourteen they were children, and after that they were adults, and expected to behave in exactly the same way as all the rest of the adult population.

Only a small minority of fourteen- to nineteen-year-olds continued to go to school or went to college. Also, there was very little part-time education available, especially in the case of the girls. Even for boys, day-release was a new idea and not very widespread, and most other training schemes involved evening classes three or four evenings a week, often for five to seven years. Not surprisingly, they had a very high drop-out rate.

Nearly all young people lived at home, and gave their parents practically all their wages. (Among the few exceptions were the girls who took jobs as living-in domestic servants.) In fact, young people usually continued to live at home until they were married, which on average was not until they were twenty-five or twenty-six for the girls, and even older for the boys.

17 After the war many young women started to go ➤ out to work when they left school. They were considered "adults" at the age of 14: the word "teenager" had not been coined.

New Wealth after the War

After the war the position was totally different. For the first time, young people everywhere were beginning to have a considerable amount of money to spend. Although more and more fifteen- to eighteen-year-olds were staying on at school, many of them were taking part-time jobs, and many were also receiving large amounts of pocket money from their parents who were benefiting from the post-war prosperity. At the same time, the young people who had left school

were earning far more than ever before. In fact, their wages were going up twice as fast as the wages of adults. In addition, most young people contributed little, if anything, to their parents' household budgets, because the parents were usually able and willing to support then, and so whatever they earned was theirs to spend as they liked.

This new wealth gave young people a special, distinct place in the community. So the word "teenagers" was coined, especially to describe them and their activities. No one knows precisely who first used the word, but it may well have been some enterprising manufacturer, who foresaw the tremendous new spending capacity of young people.

Within a few years all kinds of new consumer goods were being produced especially for teenagers. Probably most obvious were the clothes and the music, but there were also such things as scooters and motor cycles. In fact, as time went on young people between the ages of fifteen and twenty-one were spending a larger proportion of all the money spent on consumer goods in Britain than at any previous period.

Clothes were naturally of particular importance. They marked out the teenagers as a distinct group, with their own special place in the community. In their extreme form, known as "Teddy Boy" fashions, which were at their most popular in the nineteen-fifties, the clothes represented an actual rebellion against the attitudes and opinions of adult society.

Music also had an enormous appeal for nearly all teenagers. In the nineteen-fifties there was "rock'n'roll", which was accompanied by extremely energetic dancing. This was followed by what was called "beat music", and then, in the early nineteen-sixties, there was the music of the Beatles and the

18 By the nineteen-sixties and -seventies "teenagers" had established a distinct group of their own and expected a certain amount of independence, which many parents found difficult to accept.
▼

Rolling Stones, with thousands of screaming fans and mass hysteria.

Mods and Rockers and Later Groups

By the nineteen-sixties two rival groups of teenagers were constantly in the news. The reason was that they always seemed to be on the look out for a chance to have a "punch up" with each other. One group was the "Mods", who dressed smartly, rode motor-scooters and hated rock music, and the other was the "Rockers", who wore leather clothes, preferred motor-cycles to scooters and liked rock music, as their name, of course, implied.

Since then there have been many distinctive groups of teenagers, such as the "skin heads", "punks" and "bikers", to mention only a few. These groups tend to have a bad name, but the teenagers who join them are mostly unemployed, and they are probably only trying to show their contempt for a society which cannot even offer them a job.

Teenage Problems

Teenagers today present several other problems. For example, the crime rate among teenagers is rising steadily, especially in the case of crimes of violence and vandalism. At the present time one third of all indictable offences are committed by young people under the age of seventeen, and more than half by people under the age of twenty-one.

Equally worrying is the number of teenagers who take drugs. A recent survey of young people leaving school in London revealed that at least one in twenty were drug-takers. Some of these people receive treatment and are able to give up the habit, but there is a desperate shortage of centres where they can be treated, especially if they are addicted to "hard drugs".

Yet another worry is the ever-increasing sexual promiscuity among teenagers. An opinion poll conducted a few years ago revealed that two thirds of teenage boys and one third of teenage girls thought that sex before marriage was not wrong. On the other hand, another poll conducted at about the same time revealed that only a quarter of all teenagers, whatever they might say, actually had sexual intercourse before they either married or reached the age of twenty.

▲ **19** Today young people can marry at 16, or 18 if they do not have their parents consent, and they have much more freedom than their parents had at a similar age.

Some blame for the teenagers' problems is undoubtedly due to the increase in divorce among their parents. (Today over a third of all marriages in England and Wales ends in divorce.) But most divorces occur when couples have only been married for two or three years, and by the time the children are teenagers the parents are generally remarried, and there is usually a stable family life once again.

Blame for teenagers' problems can also be levelled at the schools they attend. In the big cities, in particular, the schools often seem to the teenagers to be uncaring places, offering little that is apparently relevant to life today. As a result, truancy is extremely high in the upper forms (an 80 per cent attendance is usually considered satisfactory for older pupils), and the time taken off from school is sometimes spent in shop-lifting and similar unlawful activities.

On the positive side, nearly half the thirteen to sixteen year-olds today have part-time jobs. Newspaper rounds are by far the most popular, with Saturday jobs in shops coming next. This not only gives the teenagers some extra pocket money, but also work experience, and all the local authorities have strict rules to try to make sure that the young people are not exploited.

◄ **20** Young people today are becoming more socially aware. There are many voluntary schemes to help the elderly and infirm.

6
Education

State and Private Schools in the 1930s

Education in 1930 was broadly of two types. The vast majority of children went to the nearest State elementary school from the moment they had their fifth birthday. These schools were often grim, forbidding buildings, with as many as fifty children in a class, and discipline, which was strict, was usually enforced with the cane.

The better-off children, on the other hand, usually went to private schools. Although fees were sometimes as little as £3 per term, this often meant considerable sacrifice on the part of middle-class parents. But many were prepared to struggle if only to save their

21 Addington Street School string orchestra, 1935. Boys and girls would have been taught in separate classrooms.

children from the risk of catching such things as head-lice, diptheria and scarlet fever which were rife in many of the elementary schools. Not all better-off children were better educated, however. Many private schools had large classes, untrained teachers and no provision for any kind of creative activities or games. Some of the private schools, on the other hand, were extremely good, and even put into practice the "free activity methods" which were not normally found in the State primary schools until as late as the nineteen-forties or fifties.

The children who went to the elementary schools usually stayed there until they reached the school-leaving age of fourteen. Only a very small number managed to win "scholarships" to the State grammar schools at the age of eleven. In fact, about half the grammar school pupils (even more in some areas) had previously been pupils at private schools, but their parents had decided to send them to grammar schools as paying pupils as soon as they were old enough.

As the nineteen-thirties progressed, however, the situation slowly improved. There came to be more opportunity for children from elementary schools to go on to some form of secondary education. New senior and "central" schools began to be opened for children over eleven, in adition to the old grammar schools, and by 1939 only a little over one third of the nation's children were still attending elementary schools at the age of fourteen.

The Education Act of 1944

There was no decisive, nation-wide change, however, until the Education Act of 1944 was introduced. This raised the minimum school-leaving age for all children to fifteen. Perhaps equally important, it laid down that no children were to remain at an elementary school after the age of eleven, but that they must all be transferred to some kind of secondary school. The Act did not specify any particular types of secondary schools. But in practice a three-tier system developed in most areas, consisting of grammar schools, technical schools and "modern" schools. The grammar schools were for the brightest pupils and places were allocated through the 11+ examination; the technical schools were usually for the next brightest, and all the rest of the children had to go to the "modern" schools.

Almost from the start there was dissatisfaction with this system, however. Probably the main cause for complaint was that the 11+ examination was unfair. For instance, it could depend on where children lived whether they went to a grammar school. In Merionethshire one child in three gained a place, but in Surrey it was only one child in eight. Also, as time went on, people began to question the validity of the 11+. Did it really select the most intelligent children for the grammar schools? they demanded. It certainly seemed debatable, when it was discovered that many of the children who had "failed" the 11+ did better at "O" and "A" level than some of those who had "passed".

Comprehensive Schools

As a result, there was growing pressure for a "comprehensive" system of secondary education. This was already known to work well both in the United States and in Sweden. The plan was that nearly all children would go to large "neighbourhood" schools, and that children would normally only go to other schools for religious reasons (the Roman Catholics, in particular, insisted on maintaining their own schools).

The first purpose-built comprehensive school was opened at Kidbrooke, in London, in 1954. It was for girls only, and had a thirteen-form entry (approximately 1,840 pupils). Like the majority of new comprehensive schools it possessed extremely fine buildings, which included six science laboratories, nine house craft centres and five gymnasia, all on a pleasant, spacious site.

Today the vast majority of children go to comprehensive schools. (Only a few counties,

22 Compare this photograph of a typical school class today with the previous photograph.

23 Parents are encouraged to take an interest in their children's education. These mothers run a stall every Friday at the school gates to help raise money for the school.

such as Essex, still maintain grammar schools and have an 11+ exam.) These have often been criticized as being far too big and impersonal, but they do have the advantage that all the children from a family can go to the same school,instead of being segregated according to whether they have passed the 11+ examination or not.

Examinations

The main examination taken in secondary schools before the war was the General Certificate of Education. But this was far beyond the ability of the average child, because it required passes at five specific types of subjects. So after the war the system of "O" and "A" levels was introduced, which allowed children to take any number and combination of subjects that they or their teachers chose. These exams were still too academic for the majority of children, however. So in 1965 the C.S.E. (Certificate of Secondary Education), was introduced for the less able pupils. This enabled most children to gain a certificate in at least one subject, which became even more important when the school-leaving age was raised to sixteen in 1973.

Colleges and Universities

Colleges and universities have changed just as much as schools in recent years. In the nineteen-thirties children who were awarded a "minor" scholarship to go to a grammar school could later try for a "major" scholarship to go on for further education. It was extremely difficult to gain these coveted places, however, and before the war only about one child in two hundred who started at an elementary school actually went on to a university. Nevertheless, this still represented about 20 per cent of all the university students, as in the nineteen-thirties there were only some fifty thousand university places altogether. The rest of the university students came from expensive private and public schools, and their families had to pay all their tuition fees and other expenses themselves.

24 The refectory building at the University of Sussex. In the nineteen-thirties only about 20 per cent of students who went to university could get a "scholarship" place, which meant that most of the students were from well-to-do families. Today, parents are means-tested (an investigation is made of their income), and less well-off students receive a grant from the government.

After the war the demand for further education greatly increased. This was partly due to the large numbers of young men who had been in the services and who wanted to take up their studies again. But it was also due to the enormous progress that had been made in all kinds of technical subjects, and the greatly increased demand for people with advanced technical knowledge. As a result, the government designated eight colleges (later increased to ten) as special Colleges of Advanced Technology. These all ran both "sandwich" and full-time courses, and were soon concentrating almost entirely on work of university standard. In fact, their teaching was so good that following the Robbins Report in 1963 all but one of them (which was merged with a university) received charters and became independent universities.

Seven completely new universities were also set up in the nineteen-sixties. This brought the number of university places available up to 200,000 (almost four times the pre-war figure). All these new universities have attractive sites, in semi-rural positions, and most of them are experimenting with a variety of new courses and teaching methods.

Another exciting new educational project was the founding of the Open University. After a great deal of discussion and planning this finally became a reality in 1971. People of any age could apply to become students (providing they lived in the United Kingdom), without having any previous formal educational attainments, such as "O" or "A" levels.

The Open University is mainly conducted by correspondence. But the courses also include lectures on the radio and television, and lectures recorded on cassettes. In addition, there are a number of local study centres, as well as summer schools, where the students can meet their tutors and fellow students face to face.

A first degree at the Open University is always a Bachelor of Arts. This is because the courses are modular, and may include a variety of different subjects. The subjects offered are, in fact, very wide, and include many Arts subjects (but not foreign languages), Mathematics, Science, Social Science, Educational Studies and various kinds of Technology.

7
Housing

A Housing Shortage

There was a desperate shortage of houses immediately after the First World War. Soldiers returning home from the Front found it almost impossible to rent even a few rooms for their families. By the early nineteen thirties the position was beginning to improve, although a survey carried out at the time found that more than a million families still had no self-contained accommodation of their own.

New Building in the 1930s

The shortage of houses led to a rush of "speculative" building. This meant large numbers of small, semi-detached houses and bungalows, put up by any builders who happened to have a little spare capital. Unfortunately, they were often built by the side of main roads, in what was called a "ribbon development", instead of in small, friendly groups, but at least they gave many families the first home of their own.

Most of the houses built in the nineteen-thirties were quite well-designed. They usually had three bedrooms, two living-rooms, a well-planned kitchen and a small garden,

25 This family is living in one room in a converted warehouse in a northern industrial town. The year is 1933.
▼

both at the front and the back. They did not usually have a garage, as not many families had cars at that time, but there was generally a shed for the family's bikes and garden tools.

Some of these houses cost as little as £400. This meant payments of less than ten shillings a week, through a building society. This was well within the means of the average white-collar worker, who was probably earning £4-5 a week, and even of some of the better-paid manual workers.

Poorer Housing in the 1930s

It was still far too dear for the average working-class family, however. In fact, the best that most of these families could hope for was a council house, but there were not nearly enough of these to meet the demand. Families were far more likely to have to rent some old-fashioned terraced house from a private landlord, or, worse still, just a few rooms in a house, which usually meant sharing the kitchen and the toilet with some of the other tenants. The position was particularly bad in

▲
26 These prefabricated houses were built during the war and were intended only as temporary accommodation. This photograph was taken in 1981 and shows that they are still being lived in.

some of the northern industrial cities. In places like Liverpool and Leeds there were thousands of "back-to-back" houses, which had been built seventy or even eighty to the hectare. And in Glasgow, where the slums were the worst in Britain, there were nearly 200,000 people living three, or even more, to a room.

The Effect of the War

The situation was just beginning to improve when the Second World War broke out. This brought all new building to a halt, as both the labour and the materials were needed for the war effort. What was more, thousands of homes were destroyed by enemy action during the war, and so once the fighting was over it was clear that housing had to have top priority.

◄ 27 Many high-rise flats proved to be a short-term solution to the housing problem. A high proportion of immigrant families were put into this type of accommodation but conditions were far from satisfactory and many blocks are being pulled down and families rehoused.

High-Rise Flats

Another scheme was to replace the old slums with high-rise flats. Some planners thought that a sixteen- or seventeen-storey building was the most economical way of housing large numbers of people. Unfortunately, in many cases, far too much emphasis was put on cheapness, and the flats had paper-thin walls, inadequate sanitation, chronic dampness and malfunctioning lifts. Also, it soon became clear that high-rise flats were far from ideal for children. They could not play in a garden (or even a street), and as a result some of the older children turned to vandalism. The problems grew worse as the flats began to deteriorate, and eventually in the nineteen-sixties and nineteen-seventies many blocks of flats were pulled down, and the families moved into other accommodation.

New Towns and Estates

Yet another scheme after the war was to build so-called "new towns". The idea was that families should be moved into new towns specially laid out in rural areas, to relieve the congestion in the cities. A typical "new town" was Crawley, in Surrey, which was only a village in 1950, but had no fewer than sixty thousand inhabitants ten years later. A variation of this was to build large new housing estates on the edges of existing towns. Aylesbury, in Buckinghamshire, for example, acquired several very big new estates. Naturally, industry had to be encouraged to move into the new towns, too, to provide work for the families who had moved there, but industry was expanding after the war, and this did not pose too many problems.

Prefabs

The government's first idea was to put up "prefabs" (short for "prefabricated houses"). Walls and roofs were mass-produced in a factory and simply assembled on the site. Some people condemned the prefabs as being far too bare and functional, although they did at least have modern kitchens and bathrooms, but others found them quite cosy, and a certain number are still standing even today.

28 The shopping centre in Crawley New Town in the nineteen-fifties. Even this looks old-fashioned today in comparison with modern "new-towns" such as Milton Keynes.

Some of the families who moved to the new towns missed their old friends and neighbours. But the gain in terms of better sanitation, cleanliness and privacy was certainly very great. Also, it was obvious that most of the children enjoyed their bright new schools, the parks and the spacious new shopping centres, and gradually the new towns built up their own community life.

Improvement Grants

Some families preferred to remain in their old homes, however. So in 1949 the government introduced a system of "improvement grants", to make the older houses more comfortable. During the next twenty years more than one and a quarter million homes were modernized, usually by installing such things as a bath, a lavatory, a damp course or a hot and cold water supply.

Problems Remain

Despite all the government's efforts, the housing problem has never really been solved, however. This is partly because a vast number of houses have to be built every year merely to replace the ones that have to be pulled down. In addition, people's ideas of what makes an acceptable home are constantly rising, and houses that would once have been considered quite adequate are now thought of as little better than slums. For example, a survey carried out in 1966 revealed that 12½ per cent of all homes still had no hot water, and nearly 15 per cent still had no bath (except in some cases a tub in the kitchen). This might have been acceptable a hundred years ago, but it is certainly not today, when most people consider even such things as refrigerators, washing-machines, televisions and telephones as necessities.

▲
29 A modern luxury development replaces the slums that used to run down the river.

Owner-Occupation

Probably the greatest change in housing since 1930 has been the startling increase in owner-occupation. When the war broke out there were still only three million owner-occupiers (in other words, about a quarter of all the householders). Today the number is well over double, and even council house tenants are given the opportunity to buy the houses they are renting, usually at far less than their true market value.

8
Food

The Nineteen-Thirties

The great majority of families in the nineteen-thirties had all they needed to eat. But there were some who lived barely above starvation level, usually because the father was out of work. Even in these families it was usually only the adults who regularly went hungry, however, as most parents were determined that, whatever happened, their children should not go without food.

Unfortunately, mothers did not always realize what kinds of food their children needed. They knew nothing about vitamins, proteins, calories and the like. So, despite all their parents' efforts, many children did suffer from malnutrition in the nineteen-thirties, because they lacked the more expensive "protective" foods, such as eggs, milk, butter and fresh fruit and vegetables.

For better-off families there was far greater variety in food in the nineteen-thirties than ever before. Almost every kind of food came in tins by this time, from baked beans and corned beef to tinned fruit. Also, new refrigeration methods on cargo ships made it possible to eat apples, oranges and pears from Australia and New Zealand in the winter, and Argentine beef and New Zealand lamb all the year round.

Wartime Shortages and Rationing

When the war came the situation suddenly changed. Better-off families found they had to be content with considerably less variety in their diet than in peace-time. But with no more unemployment, as everyone was needed for war-work, even the poorest people could usually afford to buy all the food on their ration books.

The first foods which were rationed were butter, sugar and bacon. But meat soon followed, rationed in terms of price and not weight, and then tea. Various other items were later rationed, including cheese, cooking fats, jam and tinned foods, until by 1944 more than half of all the money spent on food was spent on "rationed" items.

◄ **30** Tea has always been an important family meal. A father discusses the menu with his young daughter.

▲ **31** A housewife returns home with her spoils from the market. Shopping was still an almost daily chore because families did not have refrigerators to keep food fresh.

▲ **32** Shopping today is much easier, with the advent of self-service supermarkets. The whole family will often go and stock up once a month on tins for the store-cupboard and pre-packed meals to go in the freezer.

33 During the war, meal centres were set up which provided plain but nourishing food. Restaurants were not rationed, so the weekly allowance went a little further. ►

Many people supplemented these rations by eating out. Every factory with more than 250 employees had to have a canteen for its workers by law. There were also non-profit-making "British Restaurants", as they were called, all over the country, and these provided a plain but nourishing meal for about 1/2d.

The Nineteen-Fifties

Rationing continued in a modified form until as late as 1953. This was partly due to a world shortage of food, and partly to the ending of the wartime supplies from America. Also, such things as bananas, which had not been imported during the war as they were considered unnecessary luxuries, only returned to the shops very gradually.

By the mid-nineteen-fifties the food shops were all full again, however. Most people were in work and could afford to buy whatever they happened to fancy. But people's tastes had changed during the war, and there were also all kinds of new products available, and so the

average family's diet was not the same as it had been in the nineteen-thirties.

Although most families had more money, they did not eat more meat than before the war. However, the amount of chicken eaten was beginning to rise very rapidly as new methods of production brought down the cost. Also the consumption of sugar, bread and flour actually fell (to some extent, because of a campaign against them by nutritionists), and coffee began to replace tea, especially among the young.

The Nineteen-Sixties

By the nineteen-sixties the pattern of eating was changing, particularly in the south of England. Less than half the nation's families had a cooked breakfast by this time, as most people preferred to have just some cereal or toast. The midday meal usually consisted of only one course (except on Sundays), and the evening meal was generally eaten earlier than in the past, but was followed by a snack just before people went to bed. There was also a definite move, particularly in the South, away from the traditional "meat and two veg". The reason was partly that working mothers had little time to cook, and partly that many people had decided that lighter meals were healthier. In fact, more and more mothers were beginning to serve salads by the nineteen-sixties, rather than such things as steak and kidney pudding, and an ever-increasing number were even beginning to go to the new "health food" shops, and buying what they considered to be more natural, wholesome foods.

By the nineteen-sixties new "convenience" foods had also become very popular. These included ready-cooked meals in tins and foil, quick-frozen meat, fish and vegetables and dried soups. The reason once again was that more and more mothers were going out to work and were too busy to cook, yet at the same time they did have the money to spend on these expensive new products.

34 By the nineteen-sixties, with both parents often out working, "convenience foods" became, and have remained, popular. Meals have become less formal – nobody in this photograph even seems to notice what he or she is eating!

Present-Day Trends

The change in the pattern of eating has been much less marked in the North and in Scotland. In particular, the "meat and two veg" is almost as popular there as it was a generation ago. This is partly because it is colder in the North, and people feel more need for food, but it is also partly because families there tend to be less well-off, and so they are less inclined to change their habits and experiment. Also Continental ways of eating have far more influence on families who live in the South. Nowadays thousands of people from London and the Home Counties make regular trips across the Channel to buy food and drink at the huge Continental hypermarkets. They come back laden not only with wine, cheese and pâtisseries, but also with all kinds of Continental foods with much more subtle flavours than are usually available in Britain.

Nevertheless, people in all parts of Britain have been changing their ways of cooking recently. Such appliances as micro-wave ovens, electric spits and deep-fat fryers have all become very popular everywhere. This is either because they cook quickly and need the minimum of attention, which is important for busy working mothers, or because people think they cook evenly, with the least possible loss of weight during cooking.

London and the South-East are undoubtedly the places where the greatest number of foreign restaurants can be found. These include Chinese, Indian, Greek and Italian, and vary from very expensive eating-places to cheap "take-aways". But in the last few years foreign restaurants have also opened in the North, and many families all over the country now have a Chinese "take-away" at least once a week.

School Meals

One change in recent years has been in school meals. These began on a wide scale during the war, and continued afterwards so that mothers could still go out to work. But many authorities have now abolished them, partly because of their high cost and partly because today's children seem to prefer either a "packed lunch" from home or (when they are older) a snack from the local fish and chip shop.

9
Clothes

Men, Women and Children in the 1930s

The amount an average family spent on clothing in the nineteen-thirties was 4 shillings a week. Even allowing for the change in the value of money since then, this was clearly not very much. There was a far greater difference at this period between the clothes worn by poorer people (whether men, women or children) and the clothes of the better-off than there has been at any time since.

Men's clothes in the nineteen-thirties were a clear guide to their social position. The typical working-class father had just one cheap suit, which he wore with a shirt but no collar or tie. But better-off men not only had a suit with collar and tie for going to work, but also had flannel trousers and a tweed jacket for the weekends, and many of them also had plus-fours (wide, baggy trousers reaching to just below the knee), which had originally been designed for playing golf.

Many poor women still wore long black dresses and woollen shawls. But better-off women were wearing attractive mid-calf-length clothes, and wide-brimmed straw hats. Changes were on the way, though, as rayon (often called "artificial silk") was already on sale, and it was clear that cheap, man-made fibres might eventually bring fashionable clothes within the reach of everybody.

Children's clothes in the nineteen-thirties were much like their parents'. (Only better-off children, attending private schools, or those who went to grammar school, wore a school uniform.) The main expense for parents was shoes, as these could not be made at home like dresses and shirts, and many poorer children had to wear cheap, flimsy plimsolls, even all through the winter.

Clothes in Wartime

Wartime clothes rationing began in June 1941. It was worked on a "coupon" basis, with everyone receiving a certain number of "coupons" every year. People then had to give up, for example, one "coupon" for a pair of stockings, ten for a pair of shoes and perhaps twenty for a coat, although the exact number varied according to such things as whether the clothes were for adults or children.

Everyone was encouraged to "make do and mend" during the war. In fact, shops even began to open which would do such things as turning a coat or suit inside out to make it look new. In this way, better-of families, who had had a good stock of clothes before the war, usually managed to remain looking smart, although such things as evening dress soon disappeared, as people did not think it was patriotic to wear it in wartime.

Post-War Fashions

One of the first new fashions for men after the

35 A wartime clothing book showing the coupons that made shopping for clothes so difficult during the war.

war were the "Teddy Boy" outfits. The look was loosely based on Edwardian clothes, and was probably a reaction to wartime uniforms. The jackets were long and straight, with long velvet collars, the trousers were "drain-pipe", and the shoes either had thick crêpe soles or were the narrow, pointed kind known as "winkle-pickers". It was only teenagers or men in their early twenties who usually wore "Teddy Boy" clothes, however. By the time men had married and had families they usually dressed much as men had done in the nineteen-thirties. The main differences were that waistcoats were hardly ever worn any more and had been replaced by pullovers in colder weather, and that there was a growing tendency for braces to be replaced by belts.

The latest fashion for women after the war was called the "New Look". It was the idea of a French fashion designer named Christian Dior, and first appeared in 1947. Its main

features were mid-calf-length skirts, plunging neck-lines and tight waists, and, like the "Teddy Boy" suits, it was clearly a reaction to wartime austerity. Unlike the "Teddy Boy" clothes, it was not confined to the young, however. Within a matter of months, teenagers, mothers and grandmothers were all busy trying to lengthen their skirts. To be really in the fashion, it was also necessary to have a wide-brimmed hat and "platform" shoes (shoes with a very thick sole which were usually fastened round the ankle).

▲
36 Princess Margaret in 1948 dressed in the "New Look" that was such a welcome relief after the austerities of the war years.

New Materials

As well as new fashions, there were also new materials after the war. Nylon, which had begun as a material merely for stockings, was soon being used for everything from underclothes to dresses and shirts. It was quickly followed by numerous other man-made fibres, such as Terylene and polyester, which, like nylon, could all be washed in the new washing-machines without either shrinking or stretching, and required little or no ironing.

Designing for the Young

The greatest change in fashion undoubtedly came in the nineteen-sixties, however. For the first time, clothes were specially designed for the young, and were only later adopted (with

37 The floral print, the mini-skirt and "bell-bottoms" characterized the fashion of the nineteen-sixties. Note the shocked expression of the rather more conventionally dressed couple in the background, although the young woman is sporting a fairly short "mini".

▼

various modifications) by their parents. Mary Quant invented the mini-skirt and "hot pants" (extremely short, tight-fitting "shorts"), and John Stephen made London's Carnaby Street famous for his clothes for young men.

Jeans

The most enduring modern fashion only appeared in the early nineteen-seventies, though. This was for extremely strong denim trousers, reinforced at the seams with thick copper rivets. They were called "jeans", and had, in fact, been invented as long ago as the eighteen-fifties by an American tailor named Levi Strauss. Within a short time, everyone – fathers, mothers and children – all seemed to be wearing "jeans". They were on sale everywhere, from cheap market stalls to the most expensive London fashion-houses. Their biggest advantages, were, firstly, that they were extremely hard-wearing, and, secondly, that they were still considered fashionable (sometimes even more fashionable) when they began to fade and look worn-out.

38 By 1970 denim was all the rage.

Children's Wear Since 1960

Children's clothing did not change appreciably until about 1960. Then babies began to be dressed in one-piece stretch suits that buttoned or zipped up the front. These suits may not have been as attractive as earlier fashions for babies, but their advantage was that, however much a baby squirmed or wriggled, he still remained covered up and warm. At the same time, older children began wearing clothes more like their parents'. Also school uniform began to be worn by nearly all children, not merely those who were attending fee-paying schools. The uniform was usually quite simple, however, and generally just consisted of a checked dress, or skirt and blouse, for the girls (gym-slips had virtually disappeared even in private schools), and a shirt with a school tie, trousers and pullover for the boys.

Hats

One of the most noticeable features of clothing today is that so few people wear hats. The caps of the working men and the bowlers of the better-off men have almost completely disappeared. Most women never wear a hat either, even in church, and apart from some children at private schools, children today are very rarely seen in the panamas and felt hats, or the caps with the school badge on them, which children wore in the nineteen-thirties.

10
Leisure

The Cinema

One of the most popular leisure activities in the nineteen-thirties was going to the cinema. The "talkies" had only recently been introduced, and were still an exciting novelty. Also, the cost of going to the cinema was very low, even for those days. It was often as little as 9d in the afternoon, and not very much more in the evening.

By 1933 there were nearly five thousand cinemas in Britain. Some were only small "flea-pits", as they were nicknamed, but others were enormous, glittering theatres. Within a

39 By the nineteen-fifties, more and more families were acquiring televisions and cinema attendance was dropping fast. These children are spellbound by a Saturday morning film, but gradually even these children's shows were discontinued.
▼

▲ **40** From time to time cinemas try to encourage children back into the cinema. The Children's Film Foundation ran a special celebration in 1969 on their Silver Jubilee.

few years twenty million cinema tickets were being sold every week, although this did not actually mean that there were as many cinema-goers as this: some people went twice or even three times a week.

The popularity of the cinema continued right through the war years. In fact, in the nineteen-forties it was quite normal to see a long queue of patrons outside the cinemas before almost every performance. Even the black-out and the bombs did not stop people making their regular visits to the "pictures", and there can be no doubt that they helped to cheer people up in the grim days of the war.

By the mid-nineteen-fifties cinema attendance was beginning to drop dramatically, however. More and more families were buying television sets, and the cinemas just could not compete with the "small screen". For a time, many children continued to go to special Saturday morning shows at the cinemas, which were mainly a mixture of cowboy films and cartoons, but eventually even these were discontinued for lack of support.

Today there are barely a thousand cinemas left in Britain. Most of the others have either become Bingo halls or have just been pulled down. Moreover, 70 per cent of the people who still go to the cinema are in their teens or early twenties, and are often just looking for a "night out", rather than anxious to see any particular film.

Radio and Television

Another great family entertainment in the nineteen-thirties was the radio. By the time war broke out three out of every four families had a radio in their homes. There was far more music and far fewer talks and outside broadcasts than there are today, however, and on Sundays there were no programmes at all before midday, in case they might keep people away from church.

The world's first television service began in 1936 from Alexandra Palace, in North London. But very few families had sets, and the service came to a complete halt at the outbreak of war. When the programmes were resumed, only the better-off families had sets at first, but by the time of the Coronation, in 1952, some twenty-five million people had access to a television and were able to watch the broadcast of the Queen being crowned. By 1960 nearly all families either owned or rented a television. Moreover, the average family watched the television for over four hours a day, even though the programmes did not usually begin until early evening. The sets were still black and white, though. Coloured television was introduced only in 1967, and it was several years after that before a coloured set was cheap enough for the average family to be able to afford one.

Today there are numerous different ways of using a television set. Many families have videos, so that they can not only record programmes, but also rent films and then watch them at home. There are countless video games, which chiefly appeal to children and young people, and some children enjoy making up new games of their own.

41 During the war years listening to the radio was one of the great forms of family entertainment.

▲
42 The circus has always been a popular family outing.

Popular Music

Popular music today also owes a lot to radio and television. In the nineteen-thirties many of the favourite singers, like Gracie Fields and Harry Lauder, had begun in the music halls. But from about 1940 onwards popular music was dominated by the Americans, and singers like Glenn Miller, Frank Sinatra and Elvis Presley became just as famous in Britain as they were in their own country. Then in the nineteen-sixties there emerged a British group called the "Beatles". In a very short time they were "top of the pops" not only in Britain, but virtually all over the world. From then on numerous other British groups, such as "Duran Duran" and "Culture Club", have topped the charts everywhere, and today the British pop scene is a mixture of both British and American recordings.

The Theatre

In the nineteen-thirties the live theatre had only a rather limited appeal. Most families thought that theatre-going was too expensive, and that most of the plays were too "highbrow", anyway. It was only at Christmas-time, when most theatres put on pantomimes, that the average family would all go together, as a great treat, to the theatre.

During the Second World War the government tried to encourage the theatre. They thought it would boost people's morale, and help them to take their minds off their troubles. Companies were specially got together to perform both straight plays and variety, and many of them travelled many thousands of miles performing not only to the troops but to all kinds of war-workers.

Once the war was over, the theatre again lost a large part of its audience. Like the cinema, it found it extremely difficult to compete with the new draw of the television. But, rather surprisingly, there has been an enormous increase in amateur theatricals since the war, and nowadays even the smallest town has its amateur dramatic and operatic groups, which are usually extremely well-supported.

Evening Classes

After the war there was a surprising increase in all kinds of hobbies. There were long waiting-lists at all the colleges and institutes offering evening courses of any kind. The most popular courses were in car maintenance, upholstery and dressmaking, which enabled families to save money by doing jobs for themselves, but even such subjects as foreign languages and philosophy had their enthusiastic supporters.

Sundays

Perhaps the most noticeable change since the war, though, has been the increase of leisure pursuits on Sundays. In the nineteen-thirties even the cinemas were shut on Sundays, and a pleasure steamer that ran on Sundays in Scotland was denounced as the "Sabbath-

▲
43 Most children today spend hours in front of the television and with the advent of videos and home computer games many outdoor pastimes are being neglected.

breaker". Today, on the other hand, there is a definite move towards having all kinds of entertainment and sporting activities on a Sunday, as, for example, the Men's Finals Day at Wimbledon, which was traditionally held on a Saturday until a few years ago.

Closely linked with the belief that "Sunday is fun day" is the decline in church attendance. Virtually all the religious denominations have a much smaller Sunday attendance now than they did thirty years ago. The only sect which has managed to some extent to maintain its numbers has been the Roman Catholic Church, and even the Catholic Church now allows its members to attend Mass on Saturday evening, instead of Sunday, if they wish, in order to leave Sunday free for leisure activities.

11
Sport

The Nineteen-Thirties

Sport was just as popular in the nineteen-thirties as it is today. But there was far less opportunity for most people to take any part in organized games. One reason was that many people worked much longer hours than they do today, which left them little free time, and another was that there were not the facilities available, especially for the less well-to-do. Even children had less chance to play games than they do today. Many elementary schools, for example, had only an asphalt playground, with goalposts or cricket stumps painted on a wall. Also, out of school, many children had nowhere to play except the streets, particularly in urban areas, although there was a national campaign in the nineteen-

44 Before cars were mass-produced walking and hiking were popular family pastimes.

thirties to try to provide more playing-fields for young people.

Nevertheless, there were some outdoor activities that boomed in the nineteen-thirties. Among them were cycling and hiking, which were both relatively inexpensive and could be enjoyed by the whole family. Many people joined clubs for cyclists and hikers, and cafés where they could get a simple meal, or even hostels where they could stay for a night, began to be opened everywhere.

Although not strictly a sport, gardening also became immensely popular in the nineteen-thirties. Countless families had just moved to new estates where they usually had a garden of their own for the first time. One of the first people on the radio who ever had a huge personal following, running into many millions, was a broadcaster called Mr Middleton, who gave gardening hints and advice.

Spectator Sports in the 1930s

There was also plenty of opportunity for spectator sports in the nineteen-thirties. For example, football had an enormous following, although it was usually only men and boys, and not whole families, who went to watch. This enthusiasm was naturally increased by the new "pools", which first became popular in the nineteen-thirties. By 1938 some ten million people were sending in their coupons, at about 3 shillings for an entry, on average. Almost equally well supported was horse-racing. Although the actual attendance at the races was lower, five times as much was spent on betting on the horses as on the "pools". There was also the new sport of greyhound-racing, which was held in the evenings when most people had finished work. This had a large following, and betting on the dogs took about three times as much money as the "pools".

The Effect of the War

When the war broke out many sporting events suddenly came to an end. The government thought it would be unwise to allow great crowds to gather anywhere, in case there was an air-raid. Later, however, most sporting fixtures were resumed, although they tended to attract mainly local support, because of the difficulty of travelling far with no petrol for private motoring and a very restricted amount of public transport.

The Olympics at Wembley

Once the war was over, sport quickly returned to normal. In fact, a huge boost was given to games of all kinds when the Olympics were held at Wembley in 1948. This was, incidentally, a comparatively simple and friendly event compared with today's Olympic Games. Most of the competitors were accommodated in local schools rather than in the present-day huge Olympic "villages".

Taking Part

After the war there was a definite swing away from spectator sports, however. People wanted to take part in games themselves, and to make sure that their children could take part. This became even more pronounced in the nineteen-fifties, when people began having a shorter working week, and when the average family was more prosperous than ever before.

Swimming

One of the most noticeable changes was the increased popularity of swimming. New schools were often built with swimming baths, as well as with gyms and large playing-fields. Even small village schools often managed to get a small pool, usually with money raised in various ways by the local Parents-Teachers' Association. Today there are very few children who leave primary school without being able to swim. In fact, an increasing number can swim even before they are old enough for

▲
45 The 1948 Olympic Games held at Wembley gave a great boost to sport, which had suffered a considerable set-back during the war years, and many sports cubs and athletics tracks were opened where the whole family could exercise and have fun.

school. In many pools now there are "mother and baby" sessions, where babies only a few months old are taught to float, and take a few strokes, before they can walk.

New Sports

Apart from traditional games, like cricket and tennis, there are many new sporting activities nowadays. One of the first to become popular was karate, which originated in ancient times in the Far East. By 1968 there were more than two hundred and fifty karate clubs in Britain, and people of all ages, from five- or six-year-olds to grandparents, were attending them regularly.

Another popular new sport is wind-surfing. But the surf-boards are expensive, and it is also necessary to be within reach of a suitable stretch of water. A much cheaper activity is jogging, which was introduced to Britain from America in the late nineteen-seventies, and appeals to people of all ages.

The latest sport, which first appeared in the early nineteen-eighties, is aerobics. It is a kind of movement to music, which stresses the importance of correct breathing and of filling the lungs with air. It can be done either at home to a record-player, or in a group, and seems to be popular with women and girls of all ages, perhaps partly became it is said to be good for the figure.

▲
46 The "Green Goddess" has done much to make keeping fit fun and to show that all the family can join in.

47 Today's parks and pavements are crowded with "joggers" and this is another form of sport that the whole family can enjoy – even the dog!
▼

Not all new sports have managed to maintain their hold for long. In the nineteen-seventies, for example, skate-boarding became enormously popular with many children and teenagers. The number of accidents, though, was a cause of considerable concern to parents, and before more than a handful of skate-boarding rinks could be opened, the sport had virtually died out.

Fishing

Despite all the new sports, the most popular of all is probably the oldest. This is fishing. Some three million people go fishing regularly in Britain today, far more than take part in any other active sport. Fishing appeals to people of all ages and social classes, from the small boy with a stick and a piece of string, trying to catch tiddlers, to the Queen Mother fishing for salmon in Scotland.

Sport on TV

Not surprisingly, television is blamed for the falling attendance at many spectator sports, such as football. Most people obviously prefer watching sport in the comfort of their own homes, with their families. But television has certainly increased the number of people taking an active part in sport, because having watched, for instance, an ice-skating display or a snooker match, they decide they would like to have a go at that sport themselves.

48 Football has always been a popular spectator sport but with the recent wave of crowd violence many families have been frightened away from football grounds. Watford Football Club was one of the first to open a special "family stand" where children can watch the match undisturbed.
▼

12
Holidays

Developments in Holidays before the War

In the early nineteen-thirties only better-off people usually went away on holiday. The average working man had neither the time off from work nor the money to take his family away anywhere. But by the mid-nineteen-thirties almost one million industrial workers were being given a week's holiday with pay every year, and in 1938 the government passed a "holidays with pay" act, which extended the practice even further.

At first, most families went on holiday either by train or in a charabanc. (A charabanc was similar to a coach, except that it had a canvas, fold-down roof.) But by the late nineteen-thirties nearly one million families had their own cars, and there were also a large number of motor-bikes with side-cars in which some of the poorer families could get away.

Most families chose the seaside for their holidays. Bed and breakfast at the average resort cost only about 2/6d a night. There were also plenty of cafés, serving a meal for about 1/6d, as well as take-away fish and chip shops, although there were no self-service restaurants until several years after the war.

In 1937 there was also a completely new type of holiday available. This was a seaside holiday camp, and it was the idea of a young Canadian, Billy Butlin. For a family without a great deal of money these camps had one outstanding advantage. People knew in

49 The seaside has always been the most popular choice for the family holiday.

50 In 1937 Billy Butlin's first holiday camp opened. This enabled many poorer families who had not been able to afford to go away before to have a holiday, and there was always plenty to keep the children amused.

advance exactly how much their holiday would cost, including all their meals and entertainment.

Only comparatively wealthy families went abroad in the nineteen-thirties. The most popular places for people with children were Brittany, Belgium, Austria and Switzerland. But there was an excellent train service all over Europe, and once people had paid their fare, the prices in general were far lower on the Continent than in Britain.

Wartime

During the Second World War holidays virtually came to an end. There was no petrol for private motoring, and the train service was also severely restricted. In any case, servicemen were billeted in the seaside boarding houses, and there was barbed wire along most of the beaches. The average family was quite content if they were able to spend a few days with some relatives.

Developments after the War

Once the war was over, many people seemed determined to go on holiday again. The most popular destinations were such places as Clacton and Blackpool, which rapidly expanded to cater for all the holidaymakers. But even in 1947 fewer than six million people had even one week's paid holiday a year, and so large numbers of families had to be satisfied with day trips to the sea or the country.

By the nineteen-fifties people were more prosperous and far more of them had paid holidays. Also, far more families had cars, which gave them the freedom to go where they pleased. There was also the exciting new prospect of being able to go on holiday by air, which brought places like Spain only a two-hour flight away, instead of two days away by train.

At first, foreign holidays were severely restricted, though. The war had made great demands on Britain's economy, and the government did not want too much money going abroad. So, for several years after the war, no one was allowed to take more than £35-worth of currency out of Britain, and this had to pay for everything from hotel accommodation to food (but not for travelling expenses).

Once the restrictions were lifted, the demand for foreign holidays quickly soared. There were soon travel agents in every high street, and more and more new tour operators. Then "charter flights" were introduced, which meant that planes only flew when they were fully booked, and not according to a regular schedule, and this brought down very considerably the price of holidays by air.

Foreign Resorts

The most popular place for holidays by air has always been Spain. But some families prefer resorts like Rimini, in Italy, which has miles of firm, white sand, and safe bathing. Also in the last twenty years more and more families have flown across the Atlantic, mostly to visit relatives in either the United States or Canada, or sometimes to go to such sunny places as Florida.

Self-Catering in Britain

Despite the popularity of holidays abroad, most families still prefer to stay in Britain. But there has been a very definite move away from hotel holidays in recent years, in favour of some form of self-catering. Now that labour costs are so high, people find self-catering holidays cheaper, and also many of them prefer to have more choice about what they eat and at what time.

There is a wide variety of self-catering accommodation available nowadays. Some families have a caravan which they tow behind their car, while others hire a caravan which is already at their chosen site. Then there are holiday flats, cottages, farm-houses, log cabins and house-boats, and even rooms at universities, which are often to let while the students are on vacation.

▲
51 Camping is another popular form of family holiday. It gives Dad an excuse to try his hand at cooking.

Holiday Camps

After the war, holiday camps, like Butlin's, became popular once again. In fact, some firms, such as Pontin's, even opened camps on the Continent specially for British people. But holiday camps have become rather less popular in recent years, and most of the present-day camps offer self-catering holidays as an alternative to their normal full-board arrangement.

Holidays for Young People

There were very few holidays specifically for young people before the war. People seemed to think that holidays were a time when a family should all be together. There were, however, camps for Boy Scouts and Girl Guides. In fact, the first Scout camp had been opened on Brownsea Island, near Poole, in Dorset, as early as 1907.

School outings before the war were usually only day trips. But in the prosperous nineteen-sixties it became quite commonplace to take school parties abroad for ski-ing, sightseeing or even cruising. Also, exchanges between

▲
52 With the advent of the "package holiday" travel abroad has become increasingly popular. This is a typical scene at Gatwick Airport on a Saturday during the holiday season.

British school-children and children of other nationalities are now becoming increasingly popular, and give young people the chance to see at first hand what family life is like in another country.

The first Youth Hostels in Britain were opened in 1930. They were the idea of a German Richard Schirrmann, and they had already become popular on the Continent. The hostels offered simple accommodation in areas of outstanding interest and natural beauty, and any young person over fourteen years old was welcome, providing he or she arrived either on foot or on a bicycle.

Today there are well over a quarter of a million Youth Hostellers in Britain alone. There are also nearly three hundred and fifty hostels made up of a staggering variety of types. They include a shepherd's bothy, a Norman castle, a watermill, an old life-boat shed, a converted railway station and a former public house. Many young people also go to Youth Hostels abroad nowadays. The Austrian Tyrol, the Alps, the Pyrenees and the Black Forest are all particularly popular. But wherever the Youth Hostellers go some things are the same everywhere. All the hostels provide simple, inexpensive accommodation, with simple facilities for cooking, and there is always a friendly welcome.

13
Poor Families

The Unemployed in the 1930s

In 1931 there were more than $2\frac{1}{2}$ million people unemployed. Most of them were men, and the great majority had wives and children to support. The weekly unemployment pay was only 27/3d for a married man with two children, and this in real terms was less than half what a similar family was thought to need thirty years later. Worse still, after six months, every unemployed person had to undergo a "means test". This was principally to discover if he had any relatives who could be made to contribute towards his support. As a result, many teenage sons and daughters who had jobs decided to leave home, and officially "disappeared", as they knew they might be forced to help maintain the rest of the family.

The effect of unemployment on many families was appalling. They often had to live almost entirely on bread, margarine and potatoes. Then, as time went on, they were generally forced to begin pawning their blankets and selling off items of furniture, and their position grew steadily worse every day.

Unemployment and poverty were not found all over the country. They were largely confined to the "depressed areas", which mainly meant the North-East of England and

53 In the nineteen-thirties poorer families often suffered from malnutrition because they could not afford meat or many fresh vegetables. They would fill up on bread and margarine.

South Wales. These were the parts of the country where the "old industries", such as coal-mining and cotton-spinning, were still carried on, rather than the places where new commodities, such as cars and electrical goods, were produced.

The Coming of the Welfare State

When the war broke out unemployment came to a sudden end. Everybody was needed either in the fighting line or to help with the war effort at home. But the effects of many years of desperate poverty lingered on, and many better-off families in the "safe areas" were appalled when they first saw some of the children who had been evacuated from the cities. There was child after child who had never set foot in the countryside before. Some of them were clearly undernourished, and looked thin and frail compared with the country children. Many of them had no warm clothing for the winter and wore flimsy plimsolls instead of shoes, and most pathetic of all they often had all their worldly possessions in one old paper bag.

The result was a growing agitation that there should be more help for poor families. So in 1945, while the war was still on, the "Beveridge Plan" was drawn up. This aimed at creating what was termed a "Welfare State", in which no families should be forced to go without the basic necessities of life just because they are poor.

The Beveridge recommendations were put into practice as soon as the war ended. From then on, people were assured, they would be looked after by the State "from the cradle to the grave". But even a "Welfare State" could not completely abolish poverty and, as it

54 During the war many families lost their homes and possessions. The Welfare State, which was set up just after the war, was intended to provide for the poor.

turned out, many of the Report's recommendations had to be modified in any case, because of their enormous expense.

Unemployment Returns

For most people the twenty-five years after the war were a time of great prosperity. There was never more than 2 per cent of the working population unemployed, and many families now had two wage-earners, both father and mother. As a result, things like cars, televisions, washing-machines and even foreign holidays came to be regarded as quite normal, and well within the reach of almost every family.

In the late nineteen-sixties came the first signs of a change, however. Unskilled people, in particular, began to find it increasingly difficult to get a job. Then, in the early nineteen-seventies, unemployment suddenly soared to one million, and within little more than ten years it had passed the three million mark.

As in the nineteen-thirties, unemployment has not affected the whole country equally. It is much higher in certain parts of the North and in Northern Ireland than it is in the South. But whereas in the nineteen-thirties even the people in the more prosperous areas knew that poverty and hardship existed, today there is a tendency to think that the "Welfare State" is looking after everyone. To some extent this is true, of course. It is extremely rare nowadays to see the undernourished, bare-foot urchins who were an everyday sight in the nineteen-thirties. But poverty is relative, and, in a society in which almost everyone has a car and a television, not to have these things makes a family poor, even though they may be much better-off than their parents or grandparents were.

Poverty Today

There are still some families today, however, who are poor even by pre-war standards. Many of these are the families of low-paid workers,

▲
55 Many slums were demolished and their occupants moved to new, high-rise accommodation, but often this was badly built and conditions little better than what they had known before.

who have lost their jobs in the present economic recession. This kind of worker has probably never earned enough to have any savings, and after his right to unemployment benefit is exhausted he and his family must live on supplementary benefit.

Similarly, "one-parent" families sometimes live far below the official "poverty line". (A "one-parent" family usually means a mother with one or more children but no husband.) It is estimated that there are more than one million families of this type today, largely because of the increasing number of divorces, and that approximately one and a half million children are involved. Sometimes these families receive financial support from the children's father. But, even so, the mother generally has to go to work, and because of her family ties can usually only get a very poorly paid job. Nevertheless, it often costs almost as much for a "one-parent" family to live as any other family, as things like heating are just as expensive, and, in addition, a mother often has to pay a child-minder while she goes out to work.

Yet another group of people who are often poor are the elderly. Nearly one million of them are known to be living on incomes well below the "poverty line". Unfortunately, those who earned the least while they were working, and were therefore least able to save, are also those who are least likely to have any pension (except the State retirement pension) when they become too old to work.

One encouraging sign today is the number of organizations that try to help the poor. A typical example is "Shelter", whose aim is to try to make sure that every family is adequately housed. According to "Shelter", around one million families are still living in unfit or overcrowded conditions, and "Shelter" does everything it possibly can to try to alleviate the situation.

56 One-parent families are becoming more and more common as the divorce rate continues to rise, and some children have to go "into care" because their mother or father cannot cope.

14
Immigrants

Immigrants to Britain

Britain has been a multi-ethnic society for thousands of years. Romans, Angles, Saxons, Frisians and Jutes all came before the sixth century A.D. Vikings and other northern Europeans followed in the ninth and tenth centuries. Some groups came as refugees, such as Dutch Protestants in the sixteenth century, French Huguenots in the seventeenth century and Spanish Jews in the eighteenth century. The Irish have been the largest number of foreigners to come, mainly since the seventeen-fifties.

By the nineteen-thirties, Britain was already a very mixed society. Many immigrants to the UK have come from countries that were once part of the British empire. The "Commonwealth" has continued to link many of these nations as they became independent. "Old Commonwealth" countries are those which had full independence before 1931, i.e. Canada, Australia, and New Zealand. (South Africa was once part of the Old Commonwealth, but is no longer.) Most colonies in Asia, the West Indies and Africa,

57 Some children of immigrant background face extra difficulties in UK schools. Their "mother tongue" (the language spoken by the family at home) may not be standard English. In London alone, pupils speak over 130 languages as their "mother tongue".

which became independent after the Second World War, are described as the "New Commonwealth".

Immigration has helped Britain to develop. After the Second World War, immigrants were actively encouraged to come and, in 1948, a British Nationality Act was passed giving both Old and New Commonwealth citizens the right to come to Britain to live. More workers were needed to rebuild housing damaged by the war. Workers were also needed in transport, in the new National Health Service and in factories. Thousands of Europeans as well as West Indians came to fill these jobs.

There have been non-white immigrants to Britain for centuries, but their numbers increased after the Second World War because they were encouraged to come. Their labour and skills were needed in Britain. However, blacks who came in the 1950s often faced very open discrimination. There were signs saying "NO COLOUREDS" outside some rented flats. Blacks were given, for the most part, the poorest jobs, often below their skills and qualifications. It was not until 1965 that the first Race Relations Act was passed. This made it unlawful to discriminate against people because of their colour, race or national origin in some public places. More Acts have been passed since making the laws against discrimination stronger. The Race Relations Board was set up in 1965 to receive and investigate complaints. A community Relations Commission (CRC) was set up in 1968 to encourage better racial harmony. The Commission for Racial Equality (CRE) was established in 1976, replacing both the Race Relations Board and the CRC.

Open discrimination is no longer allowed as it was in the 1950s, but, even in the mid-nineteen-eighties, blacks still face extra difficulties. Discrimination in employment, housing, education and other areas of life is still a problem.

In 1960, Britain began to limit the "free entry" of people from the Commonwealth. The first Commonwealth Immigration Act was passed and applied to *New* Commonwealth citizens only: black immigrants were being considered in a different way from whites. In 1968, a second Act was also criticized by some for treating black immigrants less favourably than whites. Another Commonwealth Immigration Act followed in 1973, and a new British Nationality Act came into force in 1983. These Acts have restricted considerably who may come to Britain and who may become British. By the early nineteen-eighties, more people were *leaving* the UK than coming to Britain to live.

Ethnic Minority Families

A common pattern amongst immigrants, especially those from the New Commonwealth, has been for men to come to Britain first. Families have followed later. The immigration laws do still allow close dependants of people already lawfully settled in the UK to come into the country.

Ethnic minority families live very much like everyone else. There are, however, some different cultural influences. These are followed by some minority families more than others.

One strong influence amongst families from the Indian subcontinent is the "joint" or "extended" family. This often means that three generations live together. In the traditional extended family, old people are highly respected and cared for by their children. Family obligations are generally important. When young people marry, a daughter becomes part of her husband's extended family. Gifts may be paid by the bride's parents to the husband's family. This "dowry" of gifts is no longer legal in India – but the tradition carries on, and amongst many Asians in Britain as well. Marriages link more than just two people: two family groups are brought together. Party because of this, there is strong pressure against divorce. The divorce rate, and the number of single and unmarried parents amongst families from the Indian subcontinent in Britain is much lower than for the population as a whole.

▲
58 Corner shops run by Asian families are familiar in some UK cities. Often many members of a family work together to run such shops and other businesses.

59 A Catholic church in West London. While church attendance in Britain has been declining amongst the general population, churches with a large West Indian and African following have been growing in numbers. These include the Pentecostal and Holiness churches and the Seventh-Day Adventists.

60 The Notting Hill Carnival takes place in London each year. Steel bands carry on the West Indian carnival tradition. Efforts are being made to increase understanding between the police and ethnic minority groups.

Chinese families are also usually very close. It is the tradition to look after each other and to care for elders. It is also the tradition to ask for help from relations when help is needed. The Chinese tend to be more reluctant than other groups to turn to outsiders or to the State.

Families from the West Indies are often very close and supportive like Asian families. However, the cultural tradition of family support is not as strong as it is with Asian families. Most people in Britain of Caribbean background are descended from Africans who were taken to the Caribbean as slaves. Slave-owners did not allow normal family life. Fathers, mothers and children were often sold to work on separate plantations. Marriage was not allowed and slave fathers were not allowed rights or duties towards their children.

Slavery was ended over a hundred years ago, but the effects are still felt. In Trinidad and other islands of the Caribbean today, about 45 per cent of children are born to parents not legally married. Some of these parents live together, but many do not. It is common for a woman to be the head and supporter of her family. For West Indian families in Britain, the proportion of children living in single-parent families is higher than for the population as a whole. There is simply a very different cultural tradition about family life, brought about by slavery.

Over 5 per cent of young people in Britain under the age of sixteen are of New Commonwealth and Pakistani background. By the mid-nineteen-eighties, about 85 per cent of these young people were born in Britain. They are not immigrants themselves, but often their parents or grandparents were.

There can be some extra conflicts for young people of immigrant background. Families may want them to follow certain traditions of the home country which the young people born here may not want to follow. An example is the Indian subcontinent tradition of arranged marriages. Many young Asian girls in Britain are happy to have their marriage arranged by their parents, but some prefer to follow the British custom of choosing their own husband. This is the kind of conflict affecting many families. Both parents and children mean well. It is simply that young people of immigrant background brought up in Britain may feel themselves divided between cultural traditions at home and those they see in Britain generally.

Glossary

Aerobics a form of physical exercise stressing the importance of correct breathing.

Back-to-back houses terrace houses which have a common wall with the houses in the street behind them.

Billet, to to place people in lodgings, usually in war-time.

Call up, to to register people so that they can be directed to some form of war-work.

Charwoman a woman hired by the hour to do odd jobs in a house, especially sweeping and scrubbing.

Conscription compulsory enrolment, usually into the armed forces.

Convenience food ready-prepared meals which usually only require heating.

Cruise a holiday on board a liner which usually calls briefly at one or more foreign ports.

Evacuation the withdrawal of people from a place considered to be dangerous.

Factory farming the intensive rearing of animals in large numbers.

Flea pits small cinemas with cheap seats, so called because the people who patronized them were usually poor and were believed to have fleas.

Ghetto originally the part of a city where Jews lived, but nowadays any area where a racial (or other kind of) minority resides.

Hard drugs drugs to which a person can become addicted.

Immigrants people who have settled in a country where they were not born.

Karate a Japanese system of unarmed combat in which the blows are struck with the hands and feet.

Means test a test to check a person's income to see whether he or she qualifies for financial or social aid from the government.

Owner-occupier a person who owns the house in which he lives

Poverty line the level of income below which a person cannot live without suffering hardship.

Rayon a synthetic material made from cellulose to resemble silk.

Real terms an assessment of costs and prices taking inflation into account.

Reserved occupation an occupation which exempts people from having to undertake war work, usually because the occupation itself is of national importance.

Ribbon development the tendency to build continuously along main roads without corresponding development in the areas lying behind the roads.

Sabbath Breaker a person who does not keep the Sabbath holy (the Sabbath is Sunday in Christian communities).

Safe areas rural areas which were thought to be safe from bombing during the war.

Sandwich course a course during which the students have industrial experience sandwiched between periods at college.

Scholarship a free or subsidized place at a fee-paying school or college.

Talkies films in which the actors and actresses can be heard speaking.

Welfare State a state in which the government aims to look after anyone who is in any kind of need.

Wind-surfing a sport involving the use of a surf-board to which a sail has been attached.

Date List

1930	Two million registered unemployed
	The first Youth Hostel in Britain opened
1931	Two and a half million unemployed
	A ten per cent cut in the salaries of civil servants and teachers
1932	Birth-rate falls to below two children per family
1933	Two and three-quarter million unemployed
	More than five thousand cinemas in Britain
1935	More than one million industrial workers have a week's paid holiday
1936	World's first television service introduced, from Alexandra Palace
1937	First Butlin's holiday camp opened
1938	One and a quarter million unemployed
	Holidays with Pay Act passed
	Only three million families own their own homes
1939	Outbreak of the Second World War
	Three-quarters of a million children evacuated from large cities
1940	Women called up
	Food rationed
1941	Clothes rationed
1944	New Education Act passed
	The 11+ examination proposed
1945	End of the Second World War
	Full employment
	Beveridge Plan drawn up
1946	Number of people engaged in agriculture down to three per cent of the work force
1947	Divorces ten times more numerous than before the war
	"New Look" fashions
1948	National Health Act introduced
	Olympic Games held in Britain
1950	Barely ten per cent of the population attend church
1951	One third of the population still living in accommodation without a bath
1952	Coronation of Queen Elizabeth II
1953	Food rationing ends
1954	First purpose-built Comprehensive School opened
1958	Race riots in Nottingham and London

1960	One car for every 9.3 people Most families have a television Legal Aid Act passed
1961	One hundred and twenty thousand immigrants arrive in Britain "Mods" and "Rockers" make news
1962	New Immigration Act passed
1963	New universities established, following the Robbins Report Self-service shops becoming common-place
1964	Infant death-rate falls below two per cent
1965	C.S.E. introduced in secondary schools
1966	More than fifteen per cent of homes still have no bath, and twelve and a half per cent no hot water
1967	Family Planning Act passed Colour television introduced in Britain
1970	One car for every 4.7 people Four times as many people going abroad for holidays as ten years earlier
1971	Unemployment rising rapidly The Open University founded "Jeans" becoming popular
1972	Divorce Reform Act passed Asians from Uganda arrive in Britain
1975	Sex Discrimination Act passed
1979	More than three million unemployed
1984	One in three marriages ends in divorce
1985	One third of all indictable offences are committed by young people under 17 years old "Shelter" says that one million families in Britain are still living in unfit conditions

Books for Further Reading

T.K. Butcher
Past into Present: Country Life
Batsford, 1970

J.C. Drummond and Anne Wilbraham
The Englishman's Food
Jonathan Cape

Alan Dures
Past into Present: The Family
Batsford, 1978

Alan and Katherine Dures
History in Focus: Poverty
Batsford, 1984

Nance Lui Fyson
Growing Up in the Second World War
Batsford, 1981

Nance Lui Fyson
Growing Up in the Post-War Forties
Batsford, 1985

Cherry Gilchrist
History in Focus: People At Work, 1930 – 1980s
Batsford, 1983

Cherry Gilchrist
Finding Out About Life in Britain in the 1930s
Batsford, 1984

Sheila Gordon
Past into Present: Holidays
Batsford, 1972

Jennifer Harris
Past into Present: The Welfare State
Batsford, 1973

Sarah Harris
Finding Out About Life in Britain in the 1950s
Batsford, 1985

Sarah Harris
History in Focus: Women At Work
Batsford, 1981

C.A.R. Hills
Growing Up in the 1950s
Batsford, 1983

Madeline Jones
Finding Out About Life in Britain in World War Two
Batsford, 1983

Freda Kelsall
How We Used To Live
Macdonald Education, 1981

Peter Lane
Past into Present: The Upper Class
Batsford, 1972

W.J. Reader
Past into Present: The Middle Classes
Batsford, 1972

Marion Sichel
Costume Reference, volumes 9 and 10
Batsford, 1979

Richard Tames
Growing Up in the 1960s
Batsford, 1983

D.J. Thomas
Past into Present: Universities
Batsford, 1973

Geoffrey Trease
This is your Century
Heinemann

R.J. Unstead
Britain in the Twentieth Century
A. & C. Black, 1974

Charles Whynne-Hammond
Past into Present: Towns
Batsford, 1976

Marjorie Wilkerson
Past into Present: Clothes
Batsford, 1974

Frances Wilkins
Growing Up between the Wars
Batsford, 1979

Christopher Wright
Past into Present: The Working Class
Batsford, 1972

Index